SÖDERBERG & SARA
CAFÉ

new Heroes&Pioneers.

Published by New Heroes & Pioneers

Photography, illustration & text: Tilde Möller and Per Söderberg
Photography page 27, 50, 90 and 115: Vanessa Hanse
Editing: Francois Le Bled
Creative direction: Francois Le Bled and Per Söderberg
Book design: Daniel Zachrisson
Copy editing: Francois Le Bled and Matt Porter

Printed and bound by Livonia (Latvia)
Legal deposit October 2020
ISBN 9789187815287

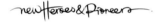

We started out as a small hole in the wall bakery, in a small town, with the vision of baking and serving stuff using local grains, no strange ingredients, as much local, free range, foraged, home grown and/or organic stuff we could get our hands on.

It all took on a life on its own as people seemed to like what we were doing, and a small hole in the wall bakery, in a small town, grew into a slightly bigger bakery, with a café, in the same small town. A coffee roastery and wood fired pizza place in the middle of nowhere. Then, a small hole in the wall bread store in a bigger town. Then we moved that into a larger old-dairy-store-turned-into-art-gallery and made a café out of it. A small piece of farmland got added to grow stuff for (mostly) the pizza place. Then we started another wood fired pizza place in the middle of a bigger town. And a pasta factory in the middle of nowhere instead of the pizza place in the middle of nowhere. And a new piece of farmland, and a gardener to take care of it.

So, now, we're stuck with:

Söderberg & Sara Bakery – Ystad, where we bake all the bread and sweet stuff, serve food and fika, pizza and natural wine and make a large amount of espresso.

Söderberg & Sara St Knut – Malmö, our big town bread store, café food-and-beverage-place. Also comes up with strange names and ideas.

Hedvigsdal Vedugn & Vin – Malmö, our wood fired pizza and natural wines (and also beer) place. Started out as a test if we could come up with new pizzas every day. It's been running for three years now, so we could.

Pastafabriken i Ingelstorp – where we make and serve fresh and dried pasta using local grains, but that is outside the scope of this book.

Two pieces of farmland, growing stuff for the above places.

This is a book that is about what we do, the things we bake and cook and serve and grow.

CHAPTER 1

STARTING WITH THREE THINGS

Flour*. Water. Salt. It was really the start of it all, as the bakery opened its doors in January 2010. We had been working at different bakeries for almost ten years, all the while, the renaissance for Swedish sourdough baking that started at the turn of the millennium was slowly picking up speed. Most (but not all) of our artisanal colleagues seemed to favour using a mixture of both baker's yeast and different types of natural leaven and we wanted to bake a bread with the simplest of ingredients. Flour, ground and milled nearby, part of it fermented into a natural leaven, high quality salt (we've been through an enormous variety of different salts since then), and water. That was the bread that would be called Folkets Levain (the People's Levain), lovingly named to reference both the former union building our bakery was located in and the Swedish habit of misusing the word Levain (just find your random French ex-pat baker living in Sweden and ask).

* Make that: Grains. Water. Salt. And maybe some dark syrup or something.

This is a weird fact: in Denmark, the rye bread is made without any
sweet stuff in it, but in Sweden we traditionally make this with a
type of molasses made from sugar beets called sirap. One time, we
tried to convert our Danish rye to a version without any syrup.
People got upset, lines of angry customers formed, threatening
emails were sent, and in a rare case of actually acting on those
types of complaints, we reverted the bread into our earlier version.
Swedish bakers, both at home and in bakeries, started baking these
types of sweet bread during some crisis or other, as flour was hard
to come by, and we discovered that syrup from the ubiquitous sugar
beet could be used in bread to prolong the storability. Apparently
we started to like it, and many types of bread in Sweden contain-
light and dark sirap.

Mörk sirap (dark syrup) is a Swedish product
made out of sugar beets. It's quite hard to
get hold of if you don't have access to
a good Scandinavian supplier — the closest
you could get is either molasses or
treacle and generally you would have to
mix light and dark. The resulting
concoction should be dark brownish
and a sweet, slightly bitter taste.

You will need a good mixer for this dough. You will also have to
be willing to experiment a bit with the baking temperature to get
things right, as every oven handles heat differently and it's criti-
cal to bake these guys for quite a long time without burning them.

You will also need a few pans capable of holding the amount of dough
while being half full, as you need space for proofing.

The dough will be very sticky, that's ok.

DANISH RYE BREAD

2 breads

Day 1
0.8 dl water
175 g crushed rye
125 g sunflower seeds
75 g flax seeds
20 g salt

Day 2
250 g rye, sifted
200 g rye, coarse
250 g rye sour dough
400 g mörk sirap, or equivalent

Mix day 1 and day 2 for about five minutes. Don't add the sirap just yet!

Let the dough rest at room temperature for about two hours.

Add the sirap, and knead in a mixer for 1 hour.

In the meantime, brush the insides of the bread pans with a neutral tasting oil.

Distribute the dough in two bread pans. Use a bowl of water to lessen the doughs tendency to stick you your hands. Flatten the dough a bit, distributing its evenly in the pans.

Proof for about two hours, aiming for the bread to rise until about 2 centimetres from the top of the trays.

Sift rye flour on top of the bread and make a diagonal cut, with a depth of about 1 centimetre. Hold the knife a bit angled.

We bake these in a stone hearth for about 1 hr at about 200°C. You probably don't, and if you do, your oven will be different from ours.

You are aiming for a baking temperature that:

A) gets the center of the bread to reach 99°C after about 1 hour - less than that and the bread will be underbaked and doughy.

B) don't burn the bread.

If the bread gets too dark too soon, open the oven to let some heat out, lower the temperature and place a baking paper on top of the bread for a while to shield the bread.

Let the bread cool completely before cutting. The bread will be a bit sticky for at least one day, so we tend to avoid selling these before properly rested.

FOLKETS LEVAIN /
THE PEOPLE'S LEVAIN

This bread has been with us since the day we opened, in the early winter of 2010, and has been our biggest seller ever since. We wanted to have a country style levain based bread with open crumb, and besides, we had been baking a lot of those kinds of bread since we stumbled into our first bakery jobs eight years before that. This bread has gone through an enormous amount of iterations since the beginnings, all with the goal of achieving a consistent open crumb, a slow fermentation process that works with the rhythm of our bakery.

Nowadays we make a stiffer sourdough out of stone milled spelt flour, as opposed to the early years of using a liquid wheat levain, to give the bread some structure. This bread also showcases our habit of adding the coarsest flour in our bread as the actual sourdough instead of using a wheat sourdough (and later on adding the coarse flour). In short and simplified: since the sourdough breaks down its own gluten, this is a way of keeping the amount of gluten available as high as possible which in turn gives us a dough that is very elastic, helping us getting the crumb as open as possible.

FOLKETS LEVAIN

1 bread

Day 1

<u>Sour dough</u>

50 g spelt flour, stone milled

0.3 dl water, luke warm

Just a wee bit of a sour dough mother

Mix everything together in a bowl with your hands. Put a lid
(or plastic) on the bowl and let stand in room temperature
for about 12 hours.

a note about sour doughs:
If you don't have any active sour dough,
there are about 1000.000 pages on the
internet about how to start one!
or you could just head down to
your local bakery and ask for
a small cup, all friendly bakeries
will want to help you with this. ♡

bakers are kind!
bakers will want
♡ to help YOU!

Day 2

450 g organic wheat flour

3.3 dl water

12 g salt

0.2 dl additional water

Some oil for the bowl

Mix flour and water for three minutes in a dough mixer on a slow gear.
Let it rest for one hour.

Add the sourdough from day 1, salt and the extra water. Mix slowly for
5 minutes, and 2 minutes fast.

Put the dough in an oiled bowl. Gently massage the topside of the dough
with some oil.

Rest for 2 hours, folding it gently a few times every 30 minutes.

Pour out the dough on a floured surface. Gently fold the dough as you
would form a simple envelope out of a paper. Place with folds facing down.

Rest for 30 minutes.

Again, fold the dough, adding a bit more tension to the dough and form into an oval.

Place the shaped dough on a floured piece of linen (or kitchen towel), folds facing up.

Leave at room temperature until you notice that the fermentation process has begun.

Place in fridge for about 12 hours.

Day 3
Heat your oven to 220°C. Heat a baking sheet in the oven.

GENTLY remove the soon-to-be-bread from the linen, placing them with folds down on a floured surface.

Score the bread with a long trace from top to the bottom of bread with an angled knife.

This allows the following:

A) you cut the bread to give the crumb more opportunities to expand as the bread rises in the oven.

B) Too many too deep cuts will make the bread expand too much sideways, giving you a flat bread.

Open the oven, add a baking paper to the hot sheet. Quickly and gently place the bread on the hot sheet, using your favourite method of adding some steam if you want, keeping the oven open as little as possible. Bake the bread for about half an hour, until proper colour. We tend to bake our bread very dark with a lot of caramelisation, but you're the baker here so it's completely up to you.

Tip: We use a lot of steam when we bake, which helps with a lot of things; a shiny crust and giving the bread some extra minutes of moisture before the surface dries, stopping the expansion. Our ovens are equipped with high grade steam generators, home ovens are most often not. There are a few tricks to get around this at home, like spraying water into the oven just before you close it. A tray of water inside the oven, placed inside a short while before inserting the bread is probably gentler to the oven.

KAVRING

Wow! Quintessential Swedish sweet rye bread! These are baked with
a lot of local variations. Somewhat iconoclastic, as we are located
in the most kavring-oriented part of Sweden, our take on these old
school loaves is a bread inspired from a traditional bread made on
the island Gotland. Don't tell anyone. We found the almost antique
cylindrical pans we bake them in when we were broke and started the
bakery; they come from a shut down bakery in the city of Gothen-
burg. They were cheap, but on the other hand, we can't find new ones
and only have enough of them for 30 breads so there's always a bit
of logistical nightmare around the big Swedish holidays when everyone needs kavring for their herring.

We bake them hard to give them a crispy, almost charred exterior
which prolongs the shelf life (at home, we only sell them fresh).
Using a locally produced rape seed oil imparts a slightly nutty
taste to our version, butter would be closer to tradition. As with
the Klosterbread (see page 20), this is also a scalded rye bread,
and like with the Danish Rye (page 9), this calls for the Swedish
Mörk Sirap to be authentic. We also use sugar called Farinsocker
(which happens to be almost the same thing as sirap, only in a
slightly dryer form) that might be hard to find outside of Sweden,
but luckily, muscovado sugar works as well.

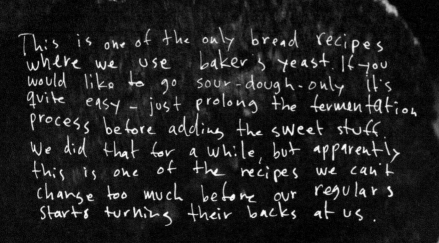

This is one of the only bread recipes
where we use baker's yeast. If you
would like to go sour-dough-only it's
quite easy – just prolong the fermentation
process before adding the sweet stuff.
We did that for a while, but apparently
this is one of the recipes we can't
change too much before our regulars
starts turning their backs at us.

2 loaves

Day 1

<u>Rye sour dough</u>
50 g stone milled rye flour
0.7 dl water
Some sourdough starter

Mix by hand until smooth. Let stand overnight at room temperature.

<u>Rye scalding</u>
3.4 dl water
155 g rye flour, stone milled
1 tsp cumin seeds

Bring the water to a boil. Add to the flour and mix with a spatula, wooden spoon or whatever you can find until the mixture is smooth and without any lumps. Cover and let it rest overnight or about 12 hours, slowly returning to room temperature.

Day 2

<u>Step 1</u>
85 g wheat flour
85 g rye flour, stone milled
25 g farin sugar (replace with muscovado, if not in Sweden)
1.5 tsp salt
0.5 dl water
8 g yeast
Rye sourdough and scalding from day 1

Mix slowly for 5 minutes. Rest 30 minutes, to get the fermentation started.

<u>Step 2</u>
190 g wheat flour
50 g dark sirap
Oil or melted butter for the pans

Add the last flour and dark sirap and mix slowly for 15 minutes. Rest for 1 hour until you see visible signs of fermentation, that is, the dough rising.

Use a lot of flour and shape loaves without folding in too much flour.

Put in greased pans. Proof until double size - in our bakery, hot from the oven, this takes about 1-2 hours.

We bake these in fully closed cylindrical pans at 280°C for about 1 hour. If baking these in regular, open pans, you might want to try 200°C for the same amount of time. The temperature inside the bread should reach 98°C, and you'll want the crust to be a very dark - not burnt - brown. Remove them from the pans and check the sides and bottom, and let them bake without pans for a few minutes more if the color is lacking!

Let cool completely before cutting the bread.

<u>Tip:</u> don't like cumin? Anis/fennel is a tested replacement. Also coffee, lingon-berries and the peels from pomerans (a form of bitter orange) works fine.

PIZZA PIZZA PIZZA

We never set out to be a Napolitan pizza place, hence, we didn't have to adhere to any rules in terms of using Italian flour (shipping in crates of 00 flour wouldn't sit well with what we're doing anyway).

We've been through lots of changes when it comes to our basic pizza dough. We always use organic flour grown and milled nearby - sometimes with ancient grains, sometimes with sour dough, sometimes without - for our pizzas, and prepare the dough in our bakery in Ystad. The oven here isn't quite as hardcore as our new one in Hedvigsdal - eyebrow and arm hair are safe with these temperatures - so this recipe works like a charm in normal home ovens too.

Before you even get started on anything else, do yourself a favour and befriend your closest flour mill. Or at the very least, the best bakery around: they can probably provide you with flour. We're not gonna get all preachy about going organic but, you know, if you want quality, you gotta go the extra mile.

Notes (find your own way)

BASIC PIZZA DOUGH

you can find a lot of info about sour dough in almost any cooking book published in the last 10 years

600 gr wheat flour
400 gr Water
60 gr wheat sour dough, levain style
12 gr salt
8 gr baker's yeast

Time to make your oven purr like a kitten on maximum temperature.

(Place flat baking tray or pizza stone inside the oven to accumulate heat)

Note: So, obviously, we get paid to geek out with dough, and having our own bakery and all the fancy gadgets needed to rock & roll the dough into pizza perfection has its perks. But there's no need to overcomplicate things at home. There are basically two ways to go about it all: you can opt for the slow, patient approach, or the fast, I-wanna-eat-like-right-now method. The slow way - the Söderberg & Sara way - which consists of proof-ing the dough in the fridge and leaving it to rest for a few days, will guarantee REALLY GOOD PIZZA DOUGH. For the need-to-satisfy-my-hunger-right-NOW method, all that is required of you is to work the dough at room temper-ature at all times. This will yield PRETTY DECENT PIZZA DOUGH with an extra brownie point: You can eat it on the SAME DAY.

time to get your hands.... floury!!

shaping edges

Knead the dough using your favourite method. What you're looking for is an elastic-but-not-too-firm dough that can be shaped easily.

Cover the dough with plastic foil or a damp kitchen towel until it starts to relax a little. We wouldn't wanna stress out our dough now, would we? If you're opting for the slow method, this is the point at which you would stick the dough into the fridge to rest overnight.

Divide the dough in four equal parts. Form the dough into balls and let it rest under cover yet again. The choice is yours: Can you wait or are you already hallucinating pizzas you're so hungry? Whatever you do: don't ever let the dough dry out. Dry parts create cracks in the dough making it hard to shape. Not that there's anything wrong with a triangle-shaped pizza but, you know - respect the authenticity and all that.

Shaping the pizza
Basic tip: Use a lot of flour on a smooth kitchen surface. There's a reason why you often see fake marble tops on pizza work surfaces: it has nothing to do with the glamorous look, and everything to do with its frictionless qualities.

Start out with a ball of dough
Now, don't think of the dough as one of those stress-balls you can squeeze and knead to your heart's content. There's actually somewhat of a system to the process. You're going to want to press your fingers into the middle of the dough and alongside the slightly raised edges. Don't be shy, get right in there! Once you've moulded the edges (the soon to be crust) to your liking, keep your fingers off - you're gonna want the edges to stay intact throughout the whole process.

Using both hands, place your fingertips along (but not on) the edge and stretch the dough by moving your hands outwards, while slowly rotating the dough and spreading your fingers - multitasking at its finest!

If the dough feels like it's getting stuck on the table, add some more flour to your work-surface before you flip the pizza upside down. As the pizza gets bigger, start using more fingers and, eventually, your whole hand, to spread the dough evenly. Maintain the slow rotation.

All the flour used? You don't want this under your pizza, so the last thing to do before sending the pizza on its way: gently lift the dough, rest it on one hand and pass it to the other a few times. This will get rid of any excess flour.

This is the stage at which baking pizza at home starts to differ from doing it at a bakery - while we have all the tools of the trade - wooden peel for pizza-to-oven transport, aluminum peel for turning and taking it out, and most importantly of all, an aggressively warm wood fired oven that will burn the hairs off your arms if you get too close to it - you probably don't. If you do: all the more power to you.

home tip: Move the pizza onto a baking sheet before schmearing the base sauce on to it and topping it with cheese and other stuff. When ready, swiftly move it to the pizza stone or hot tray and pop it in the oven. Baking time depends on your oven. We bake it until the edges are just about to burn, giving it a deeply caramellized crust.

KLOSTERBRÖD /
THE MONASTERY BREAD

Also one of our early breads. Rye doughs need a lot of water to keep the bread from getting dry and crumbly, and adding boiling water to rye flour – scalding – is a traditional way of changing the properties of flour, among other great things binding more moisture in the dough. This process has a long history in Swedish baking. Monasteries are also very historical, and besides, the town where we are located is known for a monastery so we made up this name to give it a bit of faux historical weight.

In the beginning, we made this with a rye sourdough, but that made the bread a bit to acidic for what we wanted to achieve, so we swapped some stuff out and got a lighter result with a spelt flour levain.

4 loaves

Day 1
Spelt flour levain
185 g stone milled spelt flour
1.2 dl water
A bit of a sour dough mother

Mix in a dough mixer for three minutes. Place in a covered bowl at room temperature.

Rye scalding
3 dl water
140 g rye flour, coarse and stone milled

Bring the water to a boil. Add to the flour and mix with a spatula, wooden spoon or whatever you can find until the mixture is smooth and without any lumps. Cover and let it rest overnight or about 12 hours, slowly returning to room temperature.

Day 2
1 kg wheat flour
7.2 dl water
140 g rye flour, stone milled
40 g salt

Mix for 7 minutes, slowly. Rest 30 minutes.

Mix 5 more minutes, slowly.

Place in a lightly oiled bowl, patting the dough down with oil to keep it from drying.

Let rest for 3 hours, folding it gently every 30 minutes.

Pour out the dough on a floured surface. Gently fold the dough as you would form a simple envelope out of a paper. Place with folds facing down.

Let the dough rest for 30 minutes.

Again fold the dough, adding a bit more tension to the dough and making it round.

Place the shaped dough on a floured baking basket covered with linen (or kitchen towel), folds facing up.

Let stand in room temperature until you notice that the fermentation process has begun.

Place in fridge for about 12 hours.

Day 3

Heat your oven to about 220°C, not trusting us on this, since we don't know anything about your oven. Keep a baking sheet in the oven to give it some heat.

GENTLY remove the soon-to-be-bread from the basket, placing them with folds down on a floured surface.

Score the bread, like a cross. Monastery, remember.

A) you cut the bread to give the crumb more opportunities to expand when the heat from the oven makes the bread rise.

B) Too many too deep cuts make the bread expand too much sideways, giving you a flat bread.

Open the oven, add a baking paper to the hot sheet. Quickly and gently place the bread on the hot sheet, using your favourite method of adding some steam if you want, keeping the oven open as short as possible. Bake the bread for about half an hour, until proper colour. We tend too bake our bread very dark with a lot of caramelisation, but you're the baker here so it's completely up to you.

Tip: See tip on page 13.

CHAPTER 2

TOMATO FESTIVAL

Ah, tomatoes. The lifeblood of our pizza- and pasta ventures, and nowadays almost as ubiquitous in the region as the apple if you look hard enough.

We buy as much as we can get our grubby hands on during the summer and preserve them for the winter - drying them, or cooking them slowly. During the summer we take pride in having them never meeting the inside of a fridge to keep the texture of their fruity flesh intact. The philosophy here might be: fresh tomatoes should be as fresh as possible. Otherwise cook them with as much love as possible.

GAZPACHO

We tend to serve a lot of hot soup during the year. Nothing strange about
that, we're a bakery and when you are a bakery aspiring to serve food, the
first thing you start to serve is a hot soup. We went through that soup phase
many years ago, and we still serve hot soup. This however is a cold soup.
Nothing strange about that either, we make a lot of it during the summer when
it's hot outside. Hot outside, cold soup. That made sense. Just like when you
go skiing, but the other way around: it's cold outside, and then you eat hot
soup for lunch.

Don't follow this recipe too carefully. Basically you need: a lot of tomatoes, some things that makes it a bit stingy (garlic, chili, onion), some
herbs to make it interesting (parsley, celery - although about any herb would
contribute something), something acidic (we use both lemon and vinegar for
the sake of acidic balance, but that's just a wee bit annoying) and some salt
for saltiness.

Half a cucumber
About 8-10 tomatoes
1-2 cloves of garlic
0.5-1 shallot
2 stalks of celery
1 red pepper
Chili to taste, chopped
A bunch of parsley
0.5 dl olive oil
A splash or two of white wine vinegar
Juice from half a lemon
A pinch or two of salt

Chop everything into a big bowl. Blend it into a chunky bowl of soup with an
immersion blender.

Then add salt, vinegar and lemon to taste. Add the olive oil and stir. We
prefer it chunky and thick, but if it's too chunky and thick for you, just
blend a while longer and add some water. Cover with plastic and put it in the
fridge for a while. Serve cold. Maybe with ice.

You all have ice cubes with ramson lying around in the freezer since you went
foraging last spring, use those as garnish.

oatmeal porridge

What the cinnamon bun is to a Swedish fika, the oatmeal porridge, made out of rolled oats, is to the breakfast. We serve it a la minute, freshly boiled and aim for a perfect consistence; it should juuuust barely stop being runny. If you get hold of rolled spelt, or just about any grain that can be rolled (including rye), this recipe will work out just fine, just adjust the amount of water.

2 servings

2 dl rolled oats (or other grains)
2.25 dl water
A pinch of salt

Bring everything to boil and let simmer while stirring for 3 minutes.

PIZZA WITH RICOTTA AND TOMATO

Ricotta salata. Easily confused with it's creamy sibling, Ricotta. But no. Ricotta Salata is a salty, crumbly, dry, sheep cheese. Aged for a few months and makes a lovely addition to tomatoes everywhere. Can be a bit hard to get hold of, depending on where you are. Feta cheese plays in the same ballpark (if not completely the same game), so use that if in a pinch.

Marinated tomatoes
5 tomatoes
1 lemon
2 tbsp olive oil
Thyme
Salt / pepper

Pizza dough
Tomato sauce
A small handful ricotta salata
1 ball of mozzarella, sliced 1 centimetre thick

Zest all of the lemon, juice half the lemon.

Slice the tomatoes 2 centimetres thick.

Mix everything along with some thyme, salt & pepper in a bowl.

Prepare dough with tomato sauce and 5 slices of mozzarella.

Bake it, adding the marinated lemons and the ricotta salata afterwards.

Olive oil, salt & pepper to taste.

TOMATO SAUCE.

Pizza is all about tomatoes. Or at least, it seemed like that five years ago.
We didn't know much, but we knew we would need a lot of tomatoes. Using tomatoes shipped in from Italy was, to us, like using Italian flour: never an option. It's not that we have anything against using Italian flour or tomatoes,
but buying Italian produce just to adhere to Italian pizza making policies in
Sweden seems a bit…well, you know. We do care about our environment. Luckily,
we quickly befriended our local tomato growers in Ingelstorp. Their tomatoes are grown without pesticides and delivered to our doorstep (sometimes we
fetch them ourselves) without ever seeing the interior of a walk-in fridge.
We make the tomato sauce ourselves, by roasting them slowly in our oven.
As we started to make a lot (we're talking tons) of sauce, we came up with
new methods almost every week: we experimented with quartering every tomato, cooking them in a pan, burning the pan, mixing the tomatoes in a kitchen
blender too small to hold the tomato contents, but mostly, we spent too much
time scrubbing burnt pans.

Our first white pizza was called Grisen - the pig. It consisted of a base
of crème fraiche, free range smoked pork belly from Olinge, slow roasted
Napa cabbage and mozzarella. The first year it seemed like the only ones who
ordered it were people in the restaurant business, but it slowly caught on
and is now a semi-permanent fixture on the menu. The full, slightly acidic
dairy collides with the fat from the pork belly in a lovely way, but it also
works well when a fatty punch is needed for pizzas with vegetables, herbs and
greens. Whisking the crème fraiche a bit makes it easier to smear. Sometimes
we smoke it: just put it in a smoker for a few minutes (the small ones you
buy in a fishing store work real magic). Whipped cream is a good choice for
these territories too. Being a bit fatty, it almost merges with the dough and
doesn't obscure subtle flavours like spring greens.

Actually, anything you can make a spread out of is a good base for a pizza.
Since the autumn and early spring season is quite root centered in Sweden,
we use different coloured beets, root celeriac, swede and so on, in different ways. We have made spreads out of most things spreadable; herbs, roasted
celeriac, beets.

Normally we go two different directions here; green stuff, like herbs, we
blend into a pesto. Roots or more stubborn vegetables, we tend to roast or
boil until the taste develops and they become mixable. Along with the main
attraction, you will need salt, something fatty, and something acidic. Blend/
mix it until it's spreadable.

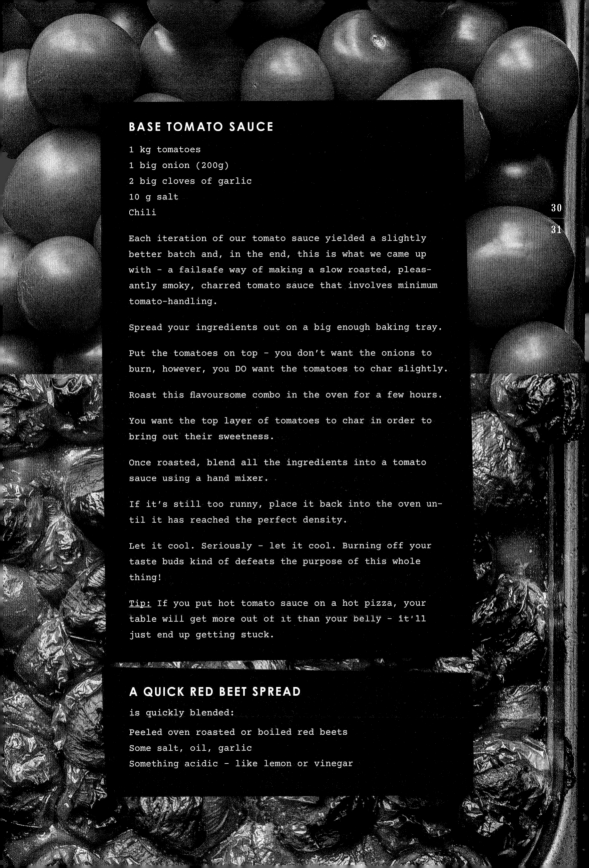

BASE TOMATO SAUCE

1 kg tomatoes
1 big onion (200g)
2 big cloves of garlic
10 g salt
Chili

Each iteration of our tomato sauce yielded a slightly better batch and, in the end, this is what we came up with - a failsafe way of making a slow roasted, pleasantly smoky, charred tomato sauce that involves minimum tomato-handling.

Spread your ingredients out on a big enough baking tray.

Put the tomatoes on top - you don't want the onions to burn, however, you DO want the tomatoes to char slightly.

Roast this flavoursome combo in the oven for a few hours.

You want the top layer of tomatoes to char in order to bring out their sweetness.

Once roasted, blend all the ingredients into a tomato sauce using a hand mixer.

If it's still too runny, place it back into the oven until it has reached the perfect density.

Let it cool. Seriously - let it cool. Burning off your taste buds kind of defeats the purpose of this whole thing!

Tip: If you put hot tomato sauce on a hot pizza, your table will get more out of it than your belly - it'll just end up getting stuck.

A QUICK RED BEET SPREAD

is quickly blended:

Peeled oven roasted or boiled red beets
Some salt, oil, garlic
Something acidic - like lemon or vinegar

PIZZA WITH TOMATO AND BURRATA

Burrata is the naughty cousin of mozzarella. A lot creamier, it's been with us for a while now. We tend to serve dishes with burrata quite uncrowded to give it some space to flaunt it's subtle sultriness.

This is one of our big sellers at Hedvigsdal. Burrata is also a staple as a starter in our pasta restaurant and a crowd pleaser on a bruschetta in our cafés.

Some basil
Olive oil
Salt / pepper
1 ball of burrata, as fresh as possible

Pizza dough
Tomato sauce
A small handful ricotta salata

Ok first of all, remove the burrata from the fridge and get it to room temperature.

Prepare dough with tomato sauce.

Bake it, tearing up the burrata in chunks over the still hot pizza.

Olive oil, salt & pepper to taste.

TOMATO BRUSCHETTA

First of all: A gentle way
to treat tomatoes.

We use a lot of tomatoes.

We use so many tomatoes that handling
all the tomatoes has it's own logistics.

LISTEN HERE: We are not even a big company, but we use about 3 tonnes of fresh tomatoes every year!

Since we get all the tomatoes fresh from the grower, we have the absolute
luxury of using tomatoes that have never been inside of a fridge. We tend to
use the tomatoes in a few different ways: we roast them for tomato sauce, we
make something sweet out of them, we use them completely fresh without anything, and we toss them with olive oil, something acidic and some herbs. This
is a good starter for something to toss them with:

About 1 dl decent olive oil
1 lemon, zest and juice
A clove of garlic, chopped
Some salt + pepper (we tend to finish with more salt and pepper so go
easy here)

Cut tomatoes in quarters, leave them to rest with the rest of the
ingredients for a few hours.

Gently marinated tomatoes
Chervil
A slice of country style sourdough bread
Salt and pepper

Tomato bruschetta with burrata

Grill a slice of the people's levain, or any other version of a country style
sour dough bread. In toaster, on stovetop, on a grill, wherever.

Place the slice of bread on a platter, add a generous amount of tomatoes.

Optional: grill the tomato sandwich in oven, with heat coming from above
until the tomatoes start to char a bit.

Put burrata on top of things.

Add more salt, pepper and chervil.

JUST ADD A

RATA

BRUSCHETTA

BURRATA!

TOMATO JAM

This is a gentle way of reminding you that botanically, the tomato is a fruit, not a vegetable. Ultra tasty on a slice of Danish rye bread with some cheese, or on your favourite porridge.

You'll need:

1 kg tomatoes
550 g sugar
Juice from 1-2 lemons

Chop the tomatoes coarsely and remove the stem. No need to cop to finely as the tomatoes will break down anyway. Add sugared lemon and boil until it thickens. We have a few tricks up our sleeves when checking if a jam is ready; one of the easiest is to pour some jam on a cool plate, dragging a spoon through it. If the jam stays divided, it's ready. If not, you obviously boil it longer.

Tip: Try adding things to this while boiling. Recommended stuff: almonds, rosemary, vanilla, bay leaves. We are quite boring though so most of the time, we keep it simple.

WHITE PIZZA WITH PICKLED TOMATOES, THYME AND GORGONZOLA

Pickled tomatoes
5 tomatoes
1 dl sugar
2 dl vinegar
3 dl water

Put oven on 50°C.

Cut tomatoes in half and put on a tray in oven for 3-4 hours, letting them dry out a bit (this is to let them soak up the pickling liquid better, just leave the drying step and dice the tomatoes if in a hurry).

Bring the pickling liquid to a boil, let it cool down.

Pur pickling liquid over tomatoes.

Pizza dough
Crème fraiche
Mozzarella
Gorgonzola, a small handful of bits and pieces
Thyme
Olive oil
Salt / pepper

Smear dough with crème fraiche and 5 slices of mozzarella, some pickled tomatoes and the gorgonzola.

Bake it, adding thyme, salt, pepper and olive oil afterwards.

CHAPTER 3

THE COW CHAPTER

A lot of what we do, and have done over the years, relates to
cows. The bakery wouldn't be what it is without a liberal use of
butter; the croissants, cinnamon buns, sandwiches and most pas-
tries. Even though we are a small bakery, compared to most other
bakeries around, we use a lot of it. No, we mean, really, a lot.
According to the nice butter person taking our orders over at
the butter company, we order more butter than any other bakery
they work with. We would never replace butter with something that
looks like butter but it's not (isn't that almost a brand name?)
although we do like some other fatty stuff: an organic cold
pressed rape seed oil from a nearby producer which we also happily use in large amounts for our doughs and some pastry stuff, and
some soft coconut butter. Now let's stop talking about butter and
talk about cheese instead.

We really do love cheese. We've made a career out of putting
cheese on stuff, like sandwiches, pizza and now pasta. We are not
religious about using local cheese although we have a few really good producers nearby, there's too many great cheeses to be
strict.

Let's list a top 5 of cheeses in order of amounts used:

Alpost from secret cheese lab *
Prästost 24 months from secret cheese lab *
Mozzarella from la treccia, Denmark
Burrata from la treccia, Denmark
A LOT of pecorino and parmigiano-reggiano, Italy

* We are one of a bunch of very happy restaurateurs/bakers to get
hold of the output from the secret cheese lab of one of the big
cheese producers in Southern Sweden. Yeah, their head cheeser
does small scale test runs of stuff that usually never reaches
the store shelves. That means anything from experiments in making
local parmesan via test runs of Swedish gruyère clones to regular
Swedish cheese staples but aged an impressive number of months,
always fun to use and always guaranteed to run out as soon as we
get fond of them.

Cultured milk stuff we use
Gräddfil, filmjölk, filbunke. And of course yogurt, crème fraiche
and kefir. Food for the baby cow, gone sour. Very exciting to
make, and we make our own cultured milk, filbunke, to serve as a
breakfast. We also use a lot of sour cream for our white pizzas.
And cream cheese for carrot/root cakes.

CAFE AU LAIT

This is not a recipe. This is just a weird story about the cups
we use.

The story goes like this.

Imagine yourself, way back in the mid eighties. Your job is, for
some reason, to get people to drink a lot of milk. You are hired
as an ad person by a milk company, that's why. Now, for some other
reason, in the last few years, people have stopped drinking as much
milk as they used to. Young people are drinking even less milk.
This makes your bosses very nervous, and it also makes you very
nervous as you know that if this continues, you will be out of
work soon. So, what do you do?

You borrow the (supposed) French way of drinking coffee with hot
milk and rebrand it, stupid. With cups adorned with Cafe au Lait in
the French tricolours. Launching it with the help of a selected few
hip and hot cafés of yesteryears and flown-in French sommeliers from
the Parisian Brasserie Lipp. The cups were then used exclusively by
the aforementioned hip cafés for a year, and then released to the
eager masses, and the lowly, not-as-hip-cafés.

And as you can always count on a Swede relating everything even
remotely French to authenticity and quality, this became quite a
big thing three decades ago and single handedly saved the declining
milk sales. Good job, imagined milk ad person!

This also led to Swedish thrift stores containing an awesome (but
dwindling - despite their porcelain looks, the cups are made of
glass and are quite fragile) treasure of these cups with we collect
and serve our CAFE AU LAITS in.

CHOCOLATE BALLS

Along with the cinnamon bun, this is the quintessential Swedish café classic!
Everyone knows how to make these, and they are the first thing you learn to
bake growing up in Sweden. When you get older you start eating factory made
chocolate balls all day at the school cafeteria, and later on it's mandatory
to eat those at every coffee break at work. This is our version. The coffee
and the toasted coconut adds a certain flair.

About 15 pieces

250 g oats
250 g butter at room temperature
125 g sugar
25 g cacao powder
25 g vanilla sugar
A shot of espresso (substitute with strong coffee)
Chocolate, chopped
Flaked or desiccated coconut

for some strange reason, instant coffee tastes great in some baked stuff.

Divide the dough in 45 gram chunks.

Roll until round and place on tray, put tray in fridge.

Meanwhile: toast coconut in oven or pan, stir often and be careful not to
burn. Let cool and transfer to a bowl.

When properly chilled, melt chocolate.

With one hand, cover the balls in a thin layer of melted chocolate. Transfer
the chocolatey balls to the bowl with coconut and cover gently.

Tip: We serve these chilled. It's perfectly acceptable to eat them at room
temperature as well, but we tend to avoid serving hand rolled things at a
temperature even remotely approaching body temp to avoid the weird feeling of
eating something directly from someone elses hands.

..... aaand it's a great idea to use one hand for the chocolate covering, and your OTHER hand for the coconut covering !! ← pro tip

CHOCOLATE AND HAZELNUT COOKIE

Let's face it. We like cows. We like butter. We like milk, we like dairy.
At one time many years ago, we promised that we would give away the key and
walk away from the bakery if something resembling margarine or any other
highly processed form of vegetable butter somehow would make its way into the
building. However, we also like vegetables, rape seed oil, oat milk, and are
eagerly awaiting the appearance of a vegan cheese that we like, so, while a
vegan croissant might never (?) become a reality in the bakery, we work with
other kinds of vegetable fatty stuff that we like. Like good tasting high
quality coconut oil in a cookie.

8 g flax seeds
8 g rye, crushed
1 dl oat milk

Grind the seeds. Mix with oat milk, and put in fridge to thicken.

1 dl coconut oil, soft
220 g sugar
150 g wheat flour
30 g cocoa
3 g bakers soda
2 g salt
75 g chocolate chips (or chopped)
75 g hazelnuts, coarsely chopped

Mix sugar and oil at fast speed for 5 minutes. Add the oat milk mixture and
continue mixing for another 5 minutes.

Sift (to avoid the flour forming lumps) and add all the dry ingredients.

toast the hazelnuts in a pan,
make sure to stir often.

Fold in chocolate chips and hazelnuts.

Scoop or form balls of dough on a tray. Put in a freezer.

Heat oven to 220°C. Bake for 10 minutes. Let cool.

FILBUNKE
SWEDISH SOUR MILK

Ok, this is old school Swedish cultured dairy, eaten since we domesticated
the cow, way back. Preferably, use unhomogenised milk for optimum creamy
goodness (although it works without it). The milk will solidify into a
pudding, eat it for breakfast or dessert.

1 l milk
2 dl yogurt
0.5 dl cream

Heat the milk to 85°C, and let it cool back to room temperature. Add yogurt
and cream. Stir, pour into bowls and refrigerate over night.

Serve with apple syrup, toasted buck wheat and cinnamon.

↑
apple syrup recipe
is on p. 131.

THE CROQUE MONSIEUR

The slightly more refined, French cousin of the grilled cheese. We use smoked ham from nearby charcuterists Södra Kompaniet for this one. We did adhere to the French habit of putting bécha-mel sauce on it, but found out it got better if we added even more cheese instead.

2 slices of sourdough bread
Butter
Dijon mustard
Cheese - we use gruyère here, but feel free to improvise.
Smoked ham

Spread butter and mustard on the bread slices. Add a few slices of ham and a big handful of grated cheese. Grill in sandwich grill, or fry in pan un-til cheese melted.

<u>A croque won't get worse if you would add:</u>

A fried egg
Some sliced tomatoes
The aforementioned sauce béchamel, on top of things
Pickled chile

GRILLED CHEESE

Cheezus christ I've written so many recipes today. I need to stop drinking coffee and get out for a while, before inside/hidden bad jokes, I-wonder-if-our-editor-will-let-this-through-or-even-discover-this-thing-I-just-wrote, and typos kill the whole project.

Grilled cheese just might be the humble king of all the grilled sandwiches. You'll need just a small amount of ingredients, and therefore you have no excuses for skimping on things.

One sandwich

2 slices of sourdough bread
Butter
Dijon mustard
Cheese! We use a mix between two Swedish classics, a 12-months grevé and a 24-months prästost. We've got absolutely no idea how to translate these cheeses, so stick to gruyère if in doubt. It's a great melter and is awesomely good.

Spread butter on both slices of bread. Don't skimp on the butter.

Spread the mustard on one of the slices. Don't skimp here either.

Grate the cheese and put a mountain of it on one of the slices. Absolutely no cheese-skimping!

Put the other slice on top, butter-side down, press and grill in your sandwich grill. If no sandwich grill, fry in a pan with a bit of butter until A) cheese melted, and B) Golden.

Cut sandwich into halves and eat.

WHITE PIZZA WITH FENNEL, GREVÉ CHEESE (*) AND TARRAGON

* You can use Emmental cheese instead

So, somewhere in the sixties, someone decided to invent a cheese in Sweden. The working name was "alp cheese" as the cheese was modeled on classics, like Gruyère. The marketing team probably decided that the name was very uncool and settled for the weird, made up, "Grevé". That doesn't mean anything in Swedish, although most Swedes believe it has something to do with the medieval title - count, as "Grevé" without the accent is a Greve, which is a Count. We also have a cheese called Baron. And Herrgård, which means "manor". And a priest cheese. And the Noble cheese. Guess you didn't know we were obsessed with the ruling class in Sweden? To add to the strangeness of Swedish cheeses, we have a gräddost, which would be translated as cream cheese, although it's not a cream cheese at all. And a rocket cheese. Please stop me.

Marinated fennel
1 bulb of fennel, very thinly sliced
Some lemon juice
A pinch of salt
Olive oil

Mix the ingredients and leave for an hour or two.

Pizza dough
Crème fraiche
A handful grated grevé cheese
Chopped tarragon
Salt / pepper

Smear dough with crème fraiche, and the cheese.

Bake it, adding fennel, tarragon, salt, pepper and some olive oil afterwards.

CHAPTER 4

EGG, BUTTER AND SUGAR

THIS CHAPTER IS ABOUT OUR SWEET STUFF (MOSTLY).

SOME RE-CIPES CONTAIN EGG, BUTTER & SUGAR. SOME MIGHT CON-TAIN ONLY ONE OR TWO OF THOSE, BUT WE THOUGHT IT WAS A GREAT NAME.

CINNAMON BUNS

Cinnamon buns, that's very Swedish, isn't it? If we were to open a bakery abroad, we would focus on cinnamon buns. And cardamom buns. Sometimes we've done pop-ups in Denmark (although it's been a while) and always sell a crazy amount of cinnamon buns.

I made this poem about cinnamon buns:

Everyone loves cinnamon buns.
Cinnamon buns make you kinder.
Cinnamon buns rely on butter.
Cinnamon buns go well with a glass of milk.
Cinnamon buns also go well with a cup of coffee.
Coffee + cinnamon buns = fika.
I wanna live with a cinnamon bun.
I could be happy the rest of my life with a cinnamon bun.
Now I feel like eating you, cinnamon bun.
Cinnamon bun, you are yummy.

There. I stole some of it from Neil Young, but I guess that's ok.

Thanks for reading my poetry. I don't know about you guys but cinnamon buns are really baked at every home here. Strangely enough, the recipes you see everywhere (like on the flour packages etc) are written by someone who would really like you to fail. If you're not living in a country where cinnamon bun recipes are everywhere, skip a few lines below. If you live in Sweden and never baked bakery style cinnamon buns before, skip forward to the spread after the next and give it a read.

<u>Kanelbulle dough</u>

Makes about 25 cinnamon buns

1.1 kg flour
200 g sugar
200 g butter (at room temperature)
5 dl milk
50 g baker's yeast
15 g coarse ground cardamom
7 g salt
1 egg

Mix all the ingredients for between 20-30 minutes, depending on preferred method.

Press the dough out to a rectangle, about 3 centimetres thick. Place under plastic in fridge for half an hour to cool down. Meanwhile:

Kanelbulle filling

250 g tempered butter
125 g muscovado or unrefined sugar
125 g sugar
Cinnamon to taste

Combine by hand or in dough mixer until it well combined. Make sure this is at room temperature well before using it, otherwise it won't spread smoothly!

Roll the dough out to a bigger rectangle (long side towards you) with a thickness of about 0.7 centimetres.

Smear a good amount of filling, covering the dough.

Fold it in thirds along the long side - first fold topmost part towards you leaving enough room to fold the downmost part away from you, creating three layers of cinnamoned/buttered dough.

Using a knife or a pizza slicer, slice the dough in parts about 2 centimetres wide.

Using your hand, roll them as the TECHNICAL DRAWING tells you.

Place them on a tray with a big amount of space between them, they will double in size when proofing.

Let proof to double size. This will take anything from about an hour upwards to 3 hours, depending on your kitchen temperature.

1 egg
Pearl sugar

Beat the eggs so that the white and egg yolks are completely mixed.

Wash with egg.

Drop a handful of pearl sugar on the bun.

Bake the buns at 200°C until golden.

Eat one bun warm. Save the rest.

Combine by hand or in dough mixer until everything is blended.
Make sure this is at room temperature well before using it.

twirl dough
around
fingers

pinchie /
time.

dough!

B

dough A
goes in
under
dough B.

A

now:
back of hand.

SEARCH: GÖRA KANELBULLE

read this in a ~~word~~ very LOUD VOICE.
Choose a voice you would listen to,
like your best teacher-getting-angry
voice!

LIST OF TRUTHS

1) Never, ever melt the butter. We know, every recipe is telling you to do that. Please don't. This would be insane. Instead, make sure the butter is at room temperature. Again: don't melt the butter.

2) There is absolutely no point in dissolving the yeast in the milk before mixing the dough. You will knead it for a really long time anyway, dissolving all the yeast nicely.

3) Don't add any more flour until you have kneaded the dough for at least 10 minutes. The dough will be sticky for a long time. The kneading will take care of that. Adding more flour too early = too much flour = dry, boring buns.

4) If kneading by hand, prepare to do it for about half an hour. At least. We mix the dough for about twenty minutes in a really effective bakery dough mixer. Read that again and ponder about that fact for a while: we mix our cinnamon doughs in a really effective professional bakery dough mixer for about twenty minutes. If you have a bit less effective dough mixer, or your own hands - add time to that. Harsh facts here!

5) We told you you would be kneading for a long time, didn't we.

6) After kneading, please refrain from proofing the dough to double its original size. We know your grandma told you so, but please don't, it will only make the dough hard to shape. Put inside refrigerator for a good rest instead.

7) In Sweden, you can find the recipe for cinnamon buns on flour packages. For some reason, the flour people decided to put them on the flour least suited for cinnamon buns. This is a trick to sell you crap flour and make you feel inferior. Always use baker's wheat flour or whatever it's called in your country.

8) NO, you don't need to use a special yeast for sweet doughs (although you could).

9) Keeping the dough cold at all times will make it easier to handle and shape.

10) When proofing, proof to double size. About double size. Underproofed buns are dry and boring and make you a dull boy/girl.

11) The buns are ready when:
    A) They got a nice colour on the topside
    B) They got a nice colour underneath.

That can take 5, 7, 8 or 13 minutes, depending on your oven. We will write 8-10 minutes, but we have absolutely no idea about how your oven works, so that's just a guess.

No one writing recipes actually know anything about what oven you have, how hot it actually is at any given temperature, or how it distributes it's heat. We just wanted to let you in on a secret: all temperatures and baking times in any book are just guesstimated lies to make you feel safe. There, now it's out in the open.

croissant.

Croissants. Flaky, delicious, not-quite-bread but not-quite pastry-like either. We use this dough for a lot of things: plain croissants, almond croissants - unlike the French Croissants aux Amandes, which commonly are made from old croissants, we bake these fresh; just fill them with almond paste, kouign-amann, Danish pastry and so on. Or bake them, leave them a day and then rebake them with almond paste if you want to be French, they are delicious that way too. Enough about almond croissants.

If you haven't spent a lot time with this kind of dough it can be daunting as the process heavily relies on keeping the butter and dough at just the right temperature at all times. A fridge and a freezer with room for the dough and a bit of patience will go a bit of the way. Some butter brands tend to break apart at lower temperatures, so feel free to blame your butter maker.

Makes about 20 croissants.

900 g wheat flour (aim for strong gluten, we make our own mix)
4 dl water, cold
90 g sugar
1 tbsp salt
40 g baker's yeast

Mix for 10 minutes in a stand mixer. You want a firm dough with a high amount of gluten.

In the meantime
500 g butter

Don't let the butter reach room temperature as this tends to make the butter break into chunks later on. Instead flatten it with a rolling pin into a square roughly the same size as the dough, about 2 centimetres thick (1).

Put into fridge.

Back to the dough
Shape it into a big ball, flatten it and immediately put into the freezer under plastic (2).

Here's the tricky part (one of them): Now you want the dough to be semi-freezed (with no icy edges) at the same time as the butter is cold enough to still be shapeable without breaking. If not, you have to come up with an idea about how to get there. It's tricky (we told you), but you are also smart and beautiful and we're sure you will figure it out.

Figured that out yet? Good. Let's proceed with the lamination on the next spread (skip part 9 if you're making kouign-amann).

When you have a sheet full of croissants (make sure they have room to expand), proof under cover at room temperature until double size. Brush CAREFULLY with a whisked egg. Bake for 18 minutes at 200°C until golden.

Tip: you can fill these with almost anything; chocolate, almond paste, almond paste and caramelised apple jam; if so, pipe the filling in between step 8 and 9.

1. flatten the piece of butter. keep it cool.

2. flatten the dough. it should also be cool.

3. place butter on dough. the width of the dough should be approx. double the width of the butter.
   fold the dough flap over the butter.

4. pinch the dough shut around the butter !

5. roll the dough. keep it rectangular and aim for a uniform thickness.

6. fold the ~~dough~~ dough so that it becomes three (3) times thicker

7. - repeat steps 5-6 one more time.
   - wrap in plastic and rest in fridge for approx 30 mins.
   - repeat steps 5-6 again.
   - flatten the dough with a rolling pin to 5mm thickness.

8. cut the dough using a sharp object (or slicer). this is the exact pattern we use.

9. roll triangular pieces to croissants. do not stretch, but keep tight.

KOUIGN-AMANN

(Traditional French bakers: avert thy eyes, this is a highly non-tradition-
al way of doing these. All others: this is ok, this is one of a handful ways
they are done in contemporary bakeries.)

This is the traditional cake from Brittany, France bearing an uncanny resem-
blance to the Danish pastry known as Spandauer. Basically, it's a combination of a laminated dough, caramelised sugar and vanilla cream, and nothing
bad would ever come out of that. The original recipes call for folding in
sugar at the laminating stage, and a lot of it. We make these with a croissant dough with liberal amounts of sugar added afterwards. You will need some
kind of cupcake sized moulds and cut baking paper to fit them. In a pinch, you
could bake these without tins/moulds, but then you would discover that the
modern kouign-amann is really just a spandau with more sugar.

Pronounce them like this and everything will be fine: *[ˌkwiɲ aˈmãn]*

Sugar
Croissant dough
Vanilla cream

Place cut-to-size papers inside cup cake tins. Sprinkle about one tbsp of
sugar on every paper.

Cut the sheet of croissant dough into squares, 10x10 centimetres.

Fold the corners of every square towards the center, like on the TECHNICAL
DRAWING. Press down in the middle to make the dough corners stay where they
are. Now you have the classical Spandau shape.

Spray the dough pieces with water and dip in sugar, covering all sides. Place
on sugared paper, in moulds. Push the dough down into the moulds.

Let proof until double sized.

Fill a piping bag with vanilla cream (check the sunshine bun recipe for
DIY piping bag tip). Stick the tip of the piping bag from the top straight
into the bun, almost but not quite to the bottom.

Pipe a generous amount of the cream into the bun.

Bake at 200°C until the sugar is caramelised - we aim for dark brown, almost
a bit brunt here. Burnt sugar = goodness.

Let cool. Eat.

10 cm

10 cm

Kouign Amann

pipe custard here

dip in sugar

This classical Portuguese pastry is surrounded by a lot of myths written about elsewhere, but as for our connection with them, we discovered them quite early in the history of our bakery during a trip to Lisbon, ate three a day and just knew we had to bring them home. They are strange and challenging beasts to make, as you bake them at a really high temperature and must come up with your own trickery to make them almost burnt at the top, the puff pastry fully baked and golden, and at the same time not let the custard like filling curdle by baking them for too long. Which is probably what makes them so much fun.

Syrup for Pastel de Nata
500 g sugar
250 g water

Heat water to dissolve the sugar.
Add Zest from 2 lemons.

Batter for about 20
100 g flour
100 g milk
Stir together

400 g milk
Bring to boil and pour over milk/flour batter while stirring vigorously.

600 g syrup
Strain the syrup to rid it from sugar crystals and add it to the mixture while stirring.

Let cool in fridge.

120 g egg yolk
90 g egg

Mix the eggs with the rest. Pour into the pastel moulds (see that recipe on the next page) and leave half a centimetre.

These are very hard to bake correctly in a home oven – the trick is to bake them hot, at least at 300°C and arrive at a well baked shell/butter dough at exactly the same time as you get burnt leopard spots on the slightly coagulated but not curdled filling. It took us about one month of experiments to arrive at 300°C heat from top and bottom, placing the sheet on three other stacked sheets and a small grate to diffuse the heat from the bottom a bit. The sweet spot, time wise, is at about 9 minutes and 20-30 seconds. Go figure. Use 300°C (if your oven goes that high) for 9 minutes as a basis for experiments and don't bake the whole batch at once.

BUTTER DOUGH
NO IT'S PUFF PASTRY!!!!

600 g wheat flour
3 dl water
10 g salt
0.5 kg cold butter

Beat the block of butter into a squared sized submission, keeping it cold.

Let the butter stand in room temperature, warming a little.

Meanwhile, mix dough for about ten minutes.

Form into a big ball of dough and rest under plastic in fridge for half an hour.

Roll the dough out to a rectangle - short side should cover the butter, long side should be double the size of the butter square.

Place butter on one side of the dough rectangle and cover with the remaining flap of dough.

Follow the croissant folding instructions (see page 65) until you have a sheet of dough folded and rolled three times.

Make rolls of the dough and store in fridge overnight.

If you are making Pastel de Nata: Cut in slices and use your thumbs to distribute the dough in the pastel moulds, be careful to not make any holes, and make sure the dough is protruding about 2-3 millimetres above the top of the moulds.

Freeze.

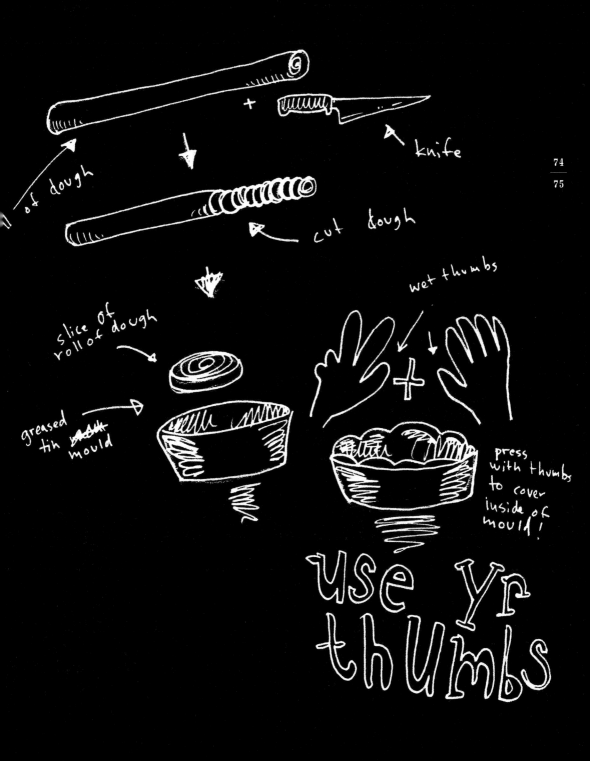

of dough

+

knife

cut dough

slice of
roll of dough

wet thumbs

greased
tin mould

+

press
with thumbs
to cover
inside of
mould!

use yr
thUmbs

Sunshine buns equals cinnamon bun dough + vanilla cream + melted butter + sugar and as you might pick up from that, they are a good thing. They are also a good thing for perfecting your one-in-each-hand-rounding moves and if you make a few thousands of them you'll be good and fast enough to be hired in a bakery, shaping round shapes.

Cinnamon bun dough
Vanilla cream
Melted butter
Sugar

Divide the cinnamon bun dough into 60 gram pieces.

Make the pieces round. The baker's way of doing this is somewhat akin to how you would rub the outside of your friend's shoulder in a circular motion with a not-quite-flat-hand. It's as easy as that but usually takes a while to learn (and is most likely totally unlearnable by reading books), so just make the pieces round in whatever way you can, placing them on a tray, ugly side down.

Proof to double size.

Fill a piping bag with vanilla cream (you can make a DIY piping bag from a small plastic bag where you cut a corner). Stick the tip of the piping from the top straight into the bun, almost but not quite to the bottom.

Pipe a generous amount of the cream into the bun.

Bake the buns until golden.

Let cool.

Wash with melted butter and cover in sugar.

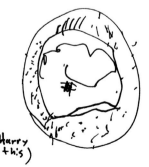

(my kid Harry
made this)

VANILLA PASTRY CREAM

1 l milk
1 vanilla pod
250 g sugar
240 g egg yolk
60 g corn starch
50 g butter

Mix the egg yolks with 200 grams each of sugar and milk, and all of the corn starch in a big bowl. Put aside.

With a knife, cut along the vanilla pod and gently scrape the insides of the pod. Put this, including the scraped bean pod along with the remaining milk and sugar in a pot and bring to a boil, stirring occasionally.

Pour the boiling milk over the egg yolk batter you made, stirring furiously.

Pour everything back into the pot and boil for about 1 minute while stirring. The mixture will thicken.

Pour the pastry cream through a strainer into a new bowl. Add the butter and stir until it has dissolved completely into the pastry cream.

BONDKAKOR
/ THE FARMER COOKIES

One thing we like with this type of cookies: you can localise them wherever
in the world you are. Local flour, local fat (wether it's grass-fed butter or
a local oil), local honey all add upp to the taste.

These cookies are part of the Swedish tradition to be able to offer a guest
seven different types of cookies at all times. We do not endorse this type of
activity as it's a silly tradition. The cookies are good though.

330 g spelt flour
2 dl sugar
1 tbsp honey
1 tsp baking soda
50 g toasted and chopped almonds
200 g room tempered butter

Mix butter, sugar and honey.

Mix spelt flour and baking soda, and sift to clear out any lumps.

Add almonds and the dry ingredients to the batter.

Work the dough until it's even.

Form two rounds, and then make them into rolls, about 4-5 centimetres thick.

Wrap in cling film and put into fridge for a few hours.

Put the oven at 200°C.

Take out the dough rolls and cut into slices with a sharp knife,
about 0.5 centimetres.

Put on sheets with paper and bake for 5-7 minutes (until golden).

SIENNAKAKA
SIENNA COOKIE

These are big sellers and have been from the beginning. They re-
semble small, floury breads, which is cool. We got this recipe from
Tina Fernlund, one of the kindest, bestest and most influential-be-
hind-the-scenes bakers in Sweden having invited probably thousands
of bakers into the bakeries she's been working or running. She
would probably tell you to add orange jam or something else with
sweet orange peels in it.

500 g almond paste
100 g farinsocker (see page 15)
75 g egg white

*farinsocker,
that's a Swedish thing again.
Use muscovado sugar instead.*

Make small round shapes, weighing in at about 15 grams. Cover in
icing sugar and put on a tray.

Bake at 200°C about 5-8 minutes. You are aiming for the surface to
caramelise into a beautiful golden-and-sugary crust, while the insides stay soft. Let cool before eating, as they will fall apart,
giving you second degree burns in the process if you touch them
while hot.

CHAPTER 5

THINGS
WE GROW

In 2015, we bought (what would be called, if you are kind) a very small farm. A field of about an acre, a small garden of apple- and plum trees and goose-berries. A run-down barn, and somewhere under a collapsed shed, a well we could use for watering. We had a long-term vision that we could grow stuff for our different spots - some rare salads, herbs and edible flowers for our new pizza place in Malmö, some vegetables, and fruit for the bakery. And also take care of some of our own food waste. Bingo!

A few years later we hired a gardener, as most of the work (and keeping the raised beds full, and harvesting stuff) is taking place exactly when the workload for us is huge elsewhere. *

Our new pasta restaurant also has a big field, so we started growing stuff there as well. A lot of basil, kale, and artichoke.

Things we are currently growing for our restaurants / the bakery: kale (a lot), dill, parsley, coriander, tomatoes (which we promptly eat ourselves most of the time), broad beans (a lot), chard and mangolds (and fodder beets, which are almost the same but for animals so the root bulb is bigger and badder - we find a strange pleasure in putting fodder beets on pizzas), juncea, bronze leaved fennel, garlic (a lot), basil (a lot), rocket/arugula in a bunch of different versions, tagetes, apples, blackberries, gooseberries, artichokes, chives

Next year maybe: zucchini flowers (for the pasta place and maybe the piz-za place), more basil (for the pasta place), more apples (for everywhere), a very big rhubarb field (for the bakery), some more trees for the long run (walnuts, pears, etc.), flowers (for the tables)

* Things we do when we should plant new stuff or harvest, in June - Aug:

this year: making a lot of pasta and pouring wine for guests

last year: making a lot of pizzas and pouring wine for guests

year before that: building another pizza place

most-of-the-time-but-not-as-often-now-because-our-bakers-are-awesome: baking a lot

all the time: driving around with a lot of tools fixing stuff that breaks

CARAMELISED APPLE JAM

A year ago, we got asked to bake a classic apple strudel for some kind of
October Fest in Malmö, and we just couldn't refuse. Per got really hyped as
he remembered a not-very-inspired strudel he was forced to bake when spending
some time at a bakery in Greece, so we decided to make the best strudel ever
made as un omaggio to Giovanni, the head baker there. Hence, Giovanni's Apfel
Strudel was invented and required enormous amounts of caramelised apple jam.
Little did we know that we had opened the flood gates of the Hoover
apfel strudel dam, and that the apfel strudel water would flow relentlessly
for many months to come, making us just stand in awe while cooking jam around
the clock.

This is somewhat similar to apple butter, but not as caramelised. We core the
apples but leave the peels on. We use it extensively, both for baked goods,
porridge and elsewhere. We use our most acidic apples in our own orchard, and
when we run out of them, we are happily located in the part of Sweden known
as the Apple Kingdom, with organic orchards within an arm's length at all
times.

400 g sugar
1 dl + 1 dl water
1.5 kg apples of a high acidic (while still being edible) variety

Core and dice the apples, leaving the peel. You'll need 1000 g of apple dices.

Caramelise the sugar and half of the water. When the sugar is brown, stop the
process by adding the rest of the water CAREFULLY, avoiding burning yourself
on sputtering sugar, which at this point is well above 100°C.

Add the apples to the pot and boil for at least 15 minutes until golden
brown. We tend to do this while doing a lot of other stuff, sometimes forgetting the apples until we pick up the smell of burnt sugar. You'll want to
turn it off at the exact point where it is caramelised and not burnt.

Can it, fridge it, or use it to make a hopelessly enormous amount of apple
strudel. You'll have to figure it out yourself though, the strudel recipe is
so complicated that we would need a whole book just to cover it.

KARAM.
ÄPPELSYLT
28/8

OATMEAL and APPLES go

hand in hand! ○ ○ ○ ○ ○ ○ ○ ○ ○ ○ ○ ○ ○ ○ ○ ○

com-
bine
{
: oatmeal porridge
: caramelized apple jam
: hazelnuts
: cinnamon
: milk

CARROT (ASSORTED ROOTS) CAKE / MOROTSKAKA

Carrot cake secrets:

A) we use a local rape seed oil with lots of taste. You should always use a local oil with lots of taste when you make carrot cake. You should always use a local oil when approaching classic recipes.

B) we tend to follow season, and food wise it get's a little depressing in the winter when all food we serve consists of different takes on beets, celeriac and carrots. HOWEVER this is the time when the carrot (assorted roots) cake really shines, as we have an endless supply of different roots to use for the cake. As we operate in the heartland of the national sugar production, we can put the raw material for our sugar - the sugar beet - to good use, by asking a kind farmer. Some roots have a somewhat annoying taste - if that's the case, just resort to a safe base amount of carrots.

270 g sugar
1.2 dl rape seed oil
140 g egg
210 g wheat flour
10 g cinnamon
1 tsp baking soda
1 tsp baking powder
1 tsp salt

200 g grated carrots
100 g grated red beets

.... or just about any combination of roots. We've been using sugar beets, parsnips, celeriac, yellow beets and many more during the years.

Whip sugar, egg and oil until light and airy.

Sift the dry ingredients to avoid lumps of flour, and add them to the batter. Mix, and gently fold in the grated roots.

Put the oven on 200°C.

Bake in a pan at 200°C for about 35 minutes. Test by putting the harmless end of a matchstick in the cake, the stick should come out clean and dry. Cake finished.

Let cool.

PLEASE do not steal sugar beets even
if it's tempting when they are lying around
roadSIDE in the autumn It's very bad,
hurtful and annoying for the farmers when
people steal the things they grow.

Frosting

125 g butter, room temperature
375 g cream cheese
100 g icing sugar, sifted
10 g vanilla sugar
Some zested lemon

Whip it all together.

Make sure the butter is tempered, sift
the icing sugar and let the cream
cheese warm to room temperature and
you'll avoid lumps.

APPLE AND HAZELNUT BUTTER SANDWICH

We like apples. We like apples so much we grow quite a lot of them, using them in everything from apple strudels to bread. This is just a good all day breakfast sandwich - for people who feel sorry for themselves - and that we only serve during the autumn on St Knut.

To make the hazelnut butter
500 g hazelnuts
1 tbsp sugar
A pinch of salt

Toast the nuts in a pan until golden.

Put everything in a blender and blitz until smooth and creamy.

Olive oil
Hazelnuts
Slice of levain style bread
Muscovado sugar
Apple, thinly sliced

Apply some oil one a slice of bread. As much as you want.

Smear a thick layer of hazelnut butter on sandwich.

Put apple slices on top, finishing with muscovado sugar to taste.

THE CIRCUS SANDWICH
/ CIRKUSMACKAN

Don't know who made up that name, or why. Must have something to do with the colours. A creation with this name can only emanate from the Malmö/St Knut crew, who tends to rename aptly named things, and then rename them again just to keep our customers, guests and not-daily staff on their toes. We need to have a talk with them about this somewhere along the line.

You really need pickled red onions and pickled lemons, otherwise it wouldn't be a circus sandwich. It would be a carrot sandwich with pickles.

Carrots, a bunch of them
Two cloves of garlic
Oil or butter, quite a lot
Salt
Pepper
Pickled lemon
Pickled red onions
Something green. Maybe micro greens or sprouts would be a good starting point. YMMV.
Some slices of levain style country bread

use pickling liquid on p. 40 to make your own.

Carrot smear thing

Slice carrots very thin, preferably with a slicer.

Chop garlic

Fry on low temperature in awesome amounts of fat, until carrots softens.

Add salt and pepper, to taste.

The sandwich

Put a healthy amount of the carrot smear thing on slice of bread. Grill in an oven with the heat coming from above until carrots start to turn lightly brown.

Add pickled lemon, pickled red onions and some green stuff.

Finish with olive oil, salt and pepper to taste.

ICED PEPPERMINT INFUSION

The easiest thing to grow might be peppermint. Just plant a
Peppermint plant somewhere where it doesn't matter if it's
taking up some space, wait a while and you will have the
tastiest weed in the world, tasting like toothpaste!

Four ingredients makes for a crisp, cooling beverage for
almost all occasions (except for some occasions).

1 l water
A handful of peppermint leaves
Half a lemon
Some honey. Preferably locally sourced etc.

Boil the water.

Rub the mint leaves in your hands a few seconds and put in
a pot along with thin slices of lemon and a big tablespoon
of honey. Pour boiling water over and let cool.

Add more lemon or honey if needed.

Serve with ice.

PASTA SALAD WITH 'NDUJA
AND HARICOT VERTS

Hand cut linguine is a very exciting shape of pasta. We prefer ours a bit thick, so it's chewy, making it perfect for pasta salad.

'Nduja is a very exciting sausage. It's originally from Calabria and is a spicy, fermented sausage which you tear open and use the inside for cooking, basically making it a sausage-without-a-sausage. Although it's perfectly acceptable to eat raw, we often tend to toast it for a while in an oven or frying pan to give it a bit more texture. The 'nduja we use is made for us by Pierre, who resides at the nearby castle of Marsvinsholm, making some of the best charcuteries we can get our hands on out of the free range pigs and wild boars roaming the domains.

130 g linguine
Some tomatoes
A bunch of haricot verts
Rocket
A few centimetres of 'nduja

in a pinch, you COULD use fresh chorizo, or some other pepper-and-pork-based sausage here.

whatever. { pork or not pork?
to pork or not to pork?
no pork is as good as pork

Some pesto (see recipe on page 114)
Lots of olive oil
Some lemon juice
Salt, Pepper

Boil pasta, following the usual advice of keeping it al dente, quickly chill it and so on.

Chop tomatoes.

Quickly blanche haricot vests in boiling water, just for one minute. If you're smart, you can figure out a way of using the pasta water for this.

Open the 'nduja and fry the contents until it gets a bit of colour and crunchiness.

Mix everything. Olive oil, lemon and salt are key players here
- as cold pasta eats a LOT of flavour.

100
101

WHITE PIZZA
WITH APPLE CHUTNEY,
SCAMORZA, ROSEMARY
AND BREADCRUMBS

Scamorza, the cheesy bacon, is a smoked mozzarella. A bit boring in itself, we combine it with stuff for a fatty smokiness that works magic with a lot of ingredients. It's a bit annoying in large amounts, so tread carefully.

Apple chutney
5 apples, with skin but not the core
1 chili, finely chopped
1 dl water
A splash of vinegar

Let boil until apples soften. Let cool a bit and mash the apples with a fork.

Pizza dough
Crème fraiche
A handful grated scamorza
A sprig of rosemary, chopped
Breadcrumbs
Salt / pepper

Smear dough with crème fraiche, the apple chutney and the scamorza.

Bake it, adding rosemary, breadcrumbs, salt, pepper and some olive oil afterwards.

WHITE PIZZA
WITH WHIPPED CREAM AND KALE

This is a recurring classic on the ever changing menu at our pizza place.
Whipped cream? Whipped cream works marvel on any pizza where you need some
fattiness to go with something acidic - this one obviously would work with
crème fraiche as well.

Marinated kale
A bunch of kale - about 500 g
2 dl olive oil
Some chopped chili, as much as you like
2 cloves of garlic
1 lemon, juiced

Mix everything but the kale with an immersion blender.

Massage mixture into kale. Let stand overnight.

Pizza dough
Whipped cream
5 slices of mozzarella
A small handful of chopped pecorino
Olive oil
Salt / pepper

Smear dough with whipped cream, and add kale and the mozzarella.

Bake it, add pecorino, salt, pepper and some olive oil afterwards.

WHITE PIZZA WITH FERMENTED CABBAGE, BROWN BUTTER AND CILANTRO

When it comes to fermenting, cleanliness is next to..... well, it's very important. Also some time and experience is a good thing!

Fermented cabbage
1 kg of cabbage, thinly sliced or shredded
20 g salt

Rub salt into the cabbage until it starts to get moist and soft.

Place in a clean glass jar with a matching lid and press the cabbage as hard as you can. When done, the cabbage/salt liquid should cover the cabbage so that no air can reach the actual cabbage. If not, add some cold water. Let stand in room temperature for about 6-7 days. Hey presto, sauerkraut!

Brown butter
You know how to make brown butter, right? If not, put some butter in a saucepan and place on medium heat. The butter will melt, and after that boil. Stir, making sure that you scrape the bottom. Aim for that distinctive point when the butter starts to smell nutty instead of like melted butter. Let cool.

Pizza dough
Crème fraiche
Mozzarella
Cilantro, a bunch
Salt / pepper

Smear dough with crème fraiche, 5 slices of mozzarella and a handful of cabbage.

Bake it, adding cilantro, salt, pepper and a generous drizzle of brown butter afterwards.

CHAPTER 6

THE FORAGING CHAPTER

The Scandinavian winter is long and dark, and in the best case - snowy.

The Scanian winter is long and dark and covered by a blanket of muddy grayness, a humid fog that arrives in November, wrapping every part of our bodies with it's depressing coldness. We walked the distance between the front door and the car, and then between the car and the bakery entrance as fast as we possibly could, all the while waiting for the next day, the next week, the next month...

Then, sometime in March, the soil slowly awakes. The nettles arrives hand in hand with the ramson and the bishop's weed, and at last you can taste the spring in the herby leaves, celebrating chlorophyll and the feeling of life slowly returning.

(Now that was very poetic.)

In Sweden, we have a thing called Allemansrätt (freedom to roam, or right to public access). Basically, that means that in Sweden all trespassing laws are out the door and we can be anywhere, picking everything we want to. Even selling it. Great, when not abused by big companies selling lingonberries picked by busloads of low-wage workers.

Most people however, treat this with a lot of respect, and most of us are brought up with at least a basic knowledge about which mushrooms are giftiga (poisonous), oätliga (inedible), goda (tasty) and utsökta (delicious) <- actual words from the standardised, subjective and slightly nonsensical scale used in every Swedish book about mushrooms.

So, we pick stuff for cooking:

* mushrooms, a lot
* elderberry flowers
* the first leaves of the elm tree
* nettles
* bishop's weed
* rowan berries
* rose hip
* blueberries and lingonberries and blackberries and wild strawberries and some other berries
* wild chervil (but please please tread carefully here as it's quite easy to confuse with the very poisonous herb called hemlock - we know where to pick chervil, if you don't, avoid)

RHUBARB
PORRIDGE

RHUBARB COMPOTE: 2 KG RHUBARB, PEELED & SLICED. 1.1KG SUGAR. 1 LEMON, ZEST AND JUICE. BOIL WHILE STIRRING UNTIL COMPOTE-Y.

} for teeeeks looks, if nothing else, use a red/purple variety if you can get hold of it!

+ chopped mint
a pinch of kosher salt
and the s&s-porridge-
ubiquitous toasted hazelnuts.
and oatmeal porridge, and milk.

porr-idge

YAY!
more porridge!

however, we do serve
large quantities of oatmeal
porridge
/ the staff
at s&s st knut.

(a tiny glass of porridge)

Porridge Porridge Porridge Porridge :||

BLUEBERRY PORRIDGE

blueberry jam.

- 2 kg blueberries
- 1.1kg sugar
- 1 lemon, juice AND zest

} boil while stirring occasionally, until 104° is reached.

cardamom/ crumble.
cinnamon

- A few leftover cinnamon buns
- Butter

tear buns apart and mix with butter. Roast in oven until crunchy. Don't burn! Yum.

—

↑ ↑ ↑

combine the above with:
- Some lemon (pickled, it's in one of ~~the~~ the pasta salad recipes)
- oatmeal porridge
- toasted hazelnuts
- milk.

MUSHROOM MIKE'S
MUSHROOM SANDWICH
/SVAMPAMICKES SVAMPAMACKA

There's this guy we call Mushroom Mike. He knows everything there is to know about edible mushrooms, and since we live in Sweden where it's socially accepted (and also not only permitted by law, but mandatory) to forage stuff almost everywhere, he gets us our mushrooms when we don't have time picking them ourselves. We also have good, local, suppliers and growers of chanterelles, oyster mushrooms and champignons so we use a lot of those, as well. It's ok to use just about any type of mushroom here.

We use a salamander broiler here to make the sandwich au gratin.
An oven would probably work too. Just keep the heat coming from above the sandwich.

A big handful of cleaned mushrooms.
A slice of levain style country bread.
Butter
Salt
Pepper
Taleggio

Heat the mushrooms with butter gently in a skillet to get rid of some moisture.

Raise the temperature and fry the mushrooms until they are brown and crisp. Add salt and pepper to taste.

Butter the slice of bread and add the mushrooms. Place cheese on top and use your favoured method of gently melting and browning the cheese.

PASTA SALAD WITH LABNEH
AND RAMSON GREMOLATA/PESTO

We make gremolata out of almost everything. The original calls for parsley, lemon and garlic though.

Mid-spring we get excited when the first ramson shows up, and we tend to use it quite a lot while others also are using it quite a lot. It's a good thing the ramson season ends before summer since it's a bit tiring on the palate with all the pestos and gremolatas tasting a lot like garlic.

ramson! ramson is a form of wild garlic and is, together with nettles, one of the first edible wild things to pop up after winter. We all get very hyped about this after spending the winter eating a lot of beets, and it wears off in about 1 month.

Gremolata/Pesto wild ramson thing

1 big bunch of parsley
1 big buch of ramson
3 lemons, zest and juice
Salt
Pepper
~5 dl olive oil

There are two directions to go here: For a gremolata, just chop things fine and omit the oil. For pesto, mix everything with an immersion blender, adding oil. If you want to keep ramson into autumn, make a pesto out of it and put in the fridge. But on the other hand, why would you,? The garlic season shows up later on, and if you spend the winter eating ramson, you wouldn't be as happy when next April brings a new bunch of ramsons.

Pickled lemon

ÄTTIKA is what we would use. Swedish Ättika is acetic acid diluted with water. Feel free to be not-as-hardcore and use a good tasting pickling liquid like rice vinegar. ←

3 sliced lemons
1/2 dl salt
1 dl sugar
2 tbsp white vinegar
1 1/2 dl water

Bring it all to a boil and pour over the lemons. This is a form of quick pickle and will keep at least a week in the fridge.

The salad

About 130 grams dried pasta
A few spoonfuls of the pesto you just made
Carrots, thinly sliced with a peeler
Pickled lemon
Labneh
Fresh ramson
Toasted buck wheat ← we use this a lot. Just toast buck wheat seeds in a pan until slightly burnt.
Salt
Pepper

Boil pasta. Use salty water. Keep it chewy. Stop the cooking process by cooling the pasta immediately.

Just mix everything together, adding salt, pepper and the toasted buck wheat to taste!

SALAD: PASTA SALAD WITH TOMATO, MOZZARELLA AND CHERVIL

```
About 130 grams of dried pasta
About two handfuls of marinated tomatoes
Half a mozzarella
A handful of rocket
Salt, pepper


Additional:

Toasted breadcrumbs
Micro greens or sprouts
Chervil.



Boil pasta. Use salty water. Keep it chewy. Stop the cooking
process by cooling the pasta immediately.

Add tomatoes and a lot of the salty vinegar and oil mixture.

Tear the mozzarella apart and add.

Add the rocket.

Fold together. Add salt if needed.

Put on a plate. Add breadcrumbs, sprouts and more chervil.

Add more salt.
```

WHITE PIZZA WITH CHANTERELLES, TALEGGIO AND BROWN BUTTER

Every Swede picks chanterelles every autumn. We also drive Volvos, believe that having a coffee and something to eat with it - the fika - is unique to Sweden, and still think the rest of the world talks about the Swedish sin, since a bunch of erotic movies were made in Sweden sometime in the sixties. Seriously, chanterelles rule.

A frying pan full of chanterelles
A slice or two of taleggio, cut into pieces
A pinch of salt for the mushrooms
Brown butter (see page 107)

Pizza dough
Crème fraiche
Just a few slices of mozzarella
A sprig or two of thyme, chopped
Salt / pepper

Fry the chanterelles, gently add first to get rid of the excess water, then at higher temperature to get the nice and brown and crispy. Add butter whenever you feel like. Add a pinch of salt.

Smear dough with crème fraiche, add the mushrooms, taleggio and mozzarella.

Bake it, adding thyme, salt, pepper and a generous drizzle of brown butter afterwards.

WHITE PIZZA WITH ´NDUJA, PICKLED ELDERBERRIES AND PECORINO

'Nduja is the famed south Italian pork sausage you can use as a spread. For this pizza we cook it though, to add some texture. We have a guy called Pierre that makes 'nduja with local free range pigs, it's really a work of marvel. If you haven't got any 'nduja-suppliers, some fresh chorizo would probably work.

'Nduja crumble

A sausage length of 'nduja

Cut open the sausage and tear it into small pieces. Add to frying pan at low/medium heat, slowly cooking it: the fat will separate and the sausage meat will start getting darker - this will take a while. Put everything in a strainer, saving the fat for something else later on.

Pickled elderberries

Half a liter of elderberries, rinsed and destemmed
1 dl sugar
2 dl vinegar
3 dl water

Bring the pickling liquid to a boil, let it cool down.

Pour pickling liquid over the elderberries.

Pizza dough
Crème fraiche
Mozzarella
A small handful pecorino
Olive oil
Salt / pepper

Smear dough with crème fraiche and 5 slices of mozzarella, and a small handful of nduja.

Bake it, adding pecorino, a spoon of elderberries, salt, pepper and olive oil afterwards.

CHAPTER 7

LEFT OVER STUFF

One of the sad truths about running a bakery: empty shelves don't pay wages, so we always have to bake a bit more than is actually sold. Think about it, if you went to a bakery in the afternoon and everything was sold out, you wouldn't come back, right? Maybe once, or twice, but then you would tire.* We are meticulously keeping statistics, keeping track of the bread we make so that we keep the potential waste minimal, but this is of course generating an amount of leftover bread every day we try to make use of to avoid wasting good (great) food!

Some of it we donate as charity for those with a less lucky disposition in life, some we sell for a symbolic price to friends running zero waste restaurants. Some we save for ourselves. The remaining part is turned into biogas and compost. As the process of fermentation and anaerobic digestion of food waste to turning it into car fuel is a big too technical even for a bunch of fermentation junkies, this chapter is all about that third part - the one we save for ourselves.

We use a lot of breadcrumbs in our restaurants, it's our secret weapon. Toasted, to bring some texture and taste to pizzas and pasta dishes, and with brown butter for desserts and cakes. It's very strange to us, but a very common question we get is "this is so good/interesting/unusual, what is it" upon the reply is "toasted breadcrumbs". Hence you get a recipe for toasted breadcrumbs to remind you that breadcrumbs rule.

* This irritating fact about the daily runnings of a bakery has led to a lot of creativity, and rumour has it that legendary French bakery owner Lionel Poilane got so upset thinking about all the bread going to waste that he started his own sandwich store, selling the open toasted sandwiches called tartines, using day old bread (with a bunch of highly creative recipes featured in the lovely book Les meilleures tartines, the only book we own). We served Tartines for a while but it got confusing as people thought it had something to know about the world famous bakery in San Francisco.

SWEET BREAD PUDDING

A forgotten old cinnamon bun, sunshine bun or just about any leftover sweet bready thing lying around can be transformed into the world's greatest sweet bread pudding if you want to. Like the casserole recipe, this is more of a way of thinking than a recipe - an endless ocean of combinations, a mere fleck of dust in deserts of food waste possibilities. You can add chocolate, toffee, jam, roasted almonds, just about any berry, cinnamon or cardamom. You can add anything! This is our basic recipe:

2, maybe 3 forgotten sweet buns
(for this one we used the sunshine bun, at page 76)
150 g blueberries

Sweet baked custard

3 dl milk
50 g sugar
1 tsp vanilla sugar

Put oven on 200°C.

Break buns into pieces, about 3 x 3 centimetres. Don't fret about the size too much. Slice the buns for a more elegant version, we prefer the more rustic approach. Mix the blueberries with the bun pieces and put in a tin lined with baking paper.

Mix the eggs with the rest of the ingredients and pour over the blueberries. Bake for about 20 minutes, or until the eggs are set and the cake has a nice, golden crust.

Let cool and put in fridge a little while. Serve with gently whipped cream.

HYPOTHETICAL CASSEROLE – CASSEROLE MADE OUT OF OLD BREAD AND ALMOST ANYTHING TASTY

This is like an inverted pie with the dough inside the pie instead of the normal way around, and also one of many of our heroes in the hunt for zero food waste.

We make ours with a lot of egg and cheese, because we like it fatty and moist. The ingredients are forever exchangeable; use any veggies, cheeses or spices you want. Basically, just dig through your fridge after leftovers and use whatever you have. This recipe is therefore completely hypothetical, only you can decide what you casserole will be like (this is quintessential Söderberg & Sara recipe behavior, and for some reason it makes our editor very upset).

Example of hypothetical casserole

You'll need:

3 thick slices of leftover sourdough bread, cut into dices
3 boiled potatoes and/or blanched broccoli and/or a bunch of fried mushrooms and/or 3 boiled red beets, in any combination and any addition sizewise resembling the 3 boiled potatoes, stated first.
1 shallot, chopped or thinly sliced
1 clove garlic, chopped or thinly sliced
250 g labneh and/or feta cheese and/or grated gruyère and/or whatever cheese-like substance you like

For the egg batter/baked custard

4 eggs
4 dl milk
Some dried chili or any spices suitable
Salt & pepa

Make the oven hot like 200°C.

Tear, split or cut your preferred vegetables into chunks. Mix bread, veggies, onion, garlic and preferred cheese in a bowl and transfer to a bread tin lined with baking paper.

Press on it a bit with your fingertips.

Mix eggs, milk and spices and pour over the veggie/cheese/tin-combination. Put in oven until the custard has solidified and the casserole has a nice colour - about 20-30 minutes.

BREADCRUMBS

We use a lot of breadcrumbs and so should you.

On pizzas.

On salads.

With brown butter and sugar as a base for
cakes, or a crumble for pies.

On pasta.

Basically everywhere where you need something
crunchy tasty to go with something that has a
soft mouthfeel.

If you have a good blender with a grating
option, that's great, that's what we use most
of the time. Just dry out left over bread in
an oven at lower temperature and grate.
Otherwise, just tear it into small chunks
before roasting. Or use a hand grater, but
that is a bit annoying,

Easiest method is to put oven at 140°C and
toast until golden and dry, quickest method
is in a frying pan, stirring often.

Blend with some browned butter for ultimate
tastiness.

CINNABUN FRENCH TOAST

We sell an awful lot o these in our Malmö café. Basically it's a French toast converted to what makes sense in Sweden - a French toast made with a cinnamon bun.

0.5 dl milk
180 g flour
2 eggs
A pinch of salt
1 tbsp sugar + more
Cinnamon
Whipped cream
Some kind of jam

You'll need a sandwich grill for this one. You could do it in a frying pan, although you would need to use butter then. Butter is good, so it would actually work out just fine.

Mix flour and eggs, then add milk. Or the other way around. That way you'll avoid lumps in the batter. Add sugar and salt.

Cut a cinnamon bun open horizontally. Dip both halves in the batter, put them together and grill until golden.

Add some more sugar, and cinnamon.

Serve immediately with whipped cream and jam.

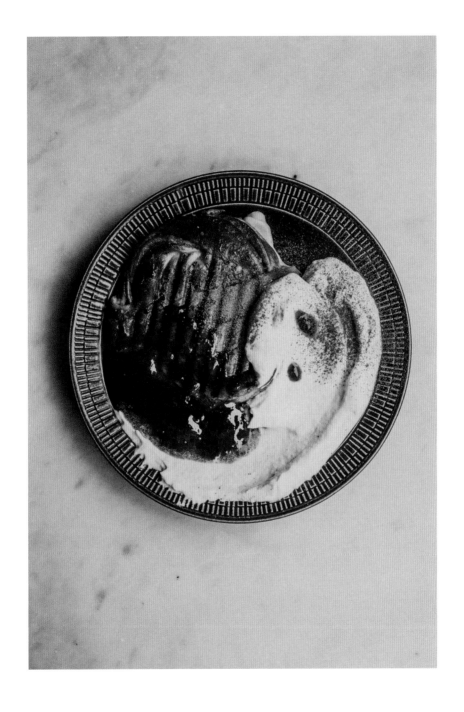

TOASTED CROISSANT FATTOUSH

Every other year, the same thing happens. One of our favourite chefs, the always inspiring Yotam Ottolenghi, comes out with a new book about vegetables and middle eastern flavours. We the enter a frenzy that lasts a few months, putting za'atar on just about everything and spend the evenings scouring the web for pomegranate syrup, or whatever else we think we need to cook like that guy.

Then things slowly go back to normal, we rediscover that sadly, no one in Ystad actually wants to eat small plates of kohlrabi with labneh and then, out of nowhere, that OTHER every other year comes around, the one where we decide that we need to put the famous Tuscan bread salad Panzanella on the menu ("We have tomatoes! We have stale bread!") forgetting that we never sell panzanella. It's one of those things that looks great on a picture, tastes good, ticks every box about sustainability by reusing that stale bread, but no one actually wants to eat (before getting upset, just calm yourself down for a minute and try to remember the last time you really, really wanted someone to sell you a panzanella. See?).

This, however, is not a panzanella, this is a fattoush. And toasted leftover croissants are way cooler than toasted stale bread.

A couple of croissants
Cucumber
Shallots
Tomato
Garlic
Mint leaves
Parsley
Olive oil
Apple syrup ←
Salt

you can easily make your own apple syrup by boiling 1l apple juice, 100 g sugar and a splash of lemon juice until thick and sticky.

Tear the croissant into small chunks. Toast in a pan until they start to dry out.

Chop everything into fitting pieces.

Mix everything together with olive oil and apple syrup - we aim for a balanced tanginess). Add salt to taste. Serve while the croissants remain crunchy.

WHITE PIZZA WITH GARLIC ROASTED COURGETTE, PECORINO, SAGE, CAPERS AND BREADCRUMBS

Yay! Breadcrumbs!

Roasted courgette
1 courgette
1 lemon, thick slices
3 cloves of garlic

Put oven on 175°C. Roast everything in oven until the courgette is really soft. Let it cool a bit, then crush it between your hands along with the garlic and a slice or two of the lemon.

Pizza dough
Crème fraiche
Mozzarella, 5 slices
1 tbsp capers, chopped
A small handful pecorino
Two sage leaves
Handful of breadcrumbs (see page 127)
Salt / pepper

Smear dough with crème fraiche, and the mozzarella.

Bake it with a large handful of courgettes on top, adding capers, pecorino, breadcrumbs, sage, salt, pepper and some olive oil afterwards.

Söderberg & Sara Ystad
Started as a small hole-in-the-wall bakery in early 2010, this
has grown into a full-size cafe, bakery, sometimes pizza place &
natural wine bar. Holder of several awards such as best bakery.

Söderberg & Sara St Knut
The little sibling of the bakery; café, bread store and neighbor-
hood hangout. Located in an old milk store in a residential area
of Malmö.

Hedvigsdal Vedugn & Vin
Our wood fired corner of Malmö Food court also serves as a popu-
lar wine bar and an experiment if we could get away with a pizza
place with an ever-changing daily menu. We could.

Pastafabriken i Ingelstorp (not featured in this book)
Country side restaurant and artisan pasta factory, where we make
pasta with Swedish produce and ancient grains.

helped us create!! Without you, no bakery, café or pizza place. Also our kids - Sixten and Harry - for putting up with us, and our parents (Thomas, Elisabeth, Åke & Inger) for always helping out during all the times of hard work and long days. You're the best!

Recipe and photo wise: extra thanks to Marcus, Agnes, Lisa, Vanessa, Arvid, Joel, and Julia for helping out with recipes and on photo occasions.

CONVERSION CHARTS

Oven Temperature Celsius (°C), Fahrenheit (°F), Gas mark (GM)

Celsius	Fahrenheit	Gas mark
110	230	1/4
120	250	1/2
135	275	1
150	300	2
160	325	3
175	350	4
190	375	5
200	400	6
220	425	7
230	450	8
245	475	9
260	500	10

Volume teaspoon (tsp), tablespoon (tbsp), millilitre (ml), liter (l), fluid ounce (fl oz)

American	Metric	Imperial
1/4 tsp	1.25 ml	
1/2 tsp	2.5 ml	
1 tsp	5 ml	
1/2 tbsp	7.5 ml	0.25 fl oz
1 tbsp	15 ml	0.5 fl oz
1/4 cup	60 ml	2 fl oz
1/3 cup	75 ml	2.5 fl oz
1/2 cup	125 ml	4 fl oz
2/3 cup	150 ml	5 fl oz
3/4 cup	175 ml	6 fl oz
1 cup	250 ml	8 fl oz
1 1/4 cup	300 ml	10 fl oz
1 1/2 cup	350 ml	12 fl oz
2 cups	500 ml	16 fl oz
2 1/2 cups	625 ml	20 fl oz
3 cups	750 ml	24 fl oz
4 cups	1 l	32 fl oz
5 cups	1.25 l	40 fl oz

Length centimetre (cm), inch (in)

Metric	Imperial
1 cm	0.3937 in
2 cm	0.8 in
3 cm	1. 2 in
4 cm	1. 6 in
5 cm	2 in
6 cm	2.4 in
7 cm	2.8 in
8 cm	3.1 in
9 cm	3.5 in
10 cm	3.9 in
20 cm	7.9 in
30 cm	11.8 in
40 cm	15.8 in
50 cm	19.7 in

Weight gram (g), kilogram (kg), ounce (oz), pounds (lbs)

Metric	US / UK
1 g	0.03527 oz
5 g	0.18 oz
10 g	0.35 oz
25 g	0.88 oz
50 g	1.76 oz
75 g	2.65 oz
100 g	3.5 oz
200 g	7.05 oz
300 g	10.58 oz
500 g	17.64 oz (1.10 lbs)
750 g	26.46 oz (1.65 lbs)
1000 g (1 kg)	35.27 oz (2.20 lbs)

All charts and recipes ingredients use approximate quantities in the conversions